101

RANCH HORSE TIPS

Other books in the series:

101 Horsekeeping Tips
101 Hunter/Jumper Tips
101 Trail Riding Tips
101 Dressage Tips
101 Reining Tips

101 Techniques for Training the Working Cow Horse
RANCH HORSE TIPS

Patrick Hooks

The Lyons Press
Guilford, Connecticut
An imprint of The Globe Pequot Press

Copyright © 2006 by Morris Book Publishing, LLC

The Lyons Press is an imprint of The Globe Pequot Press.

10 9 8 7 6 5 4 3 2 1

Printed in the United States of America

ISBN–13: 978-1-59228-878-6
ISBN–10:1-59228-878-2

The Library of Congress Cataloging-in-Publication data is available on file.

Contents

Introduction

The tips in this book are building blocks for training a ranch horse. The tips begin with working a foal at just a couple of hours old, and advance tip by tip to the basics of roping and working livestock.

As you progress from beginning to end, you will discover the similarities of the building blocks, how they complement one another, and how they revolve around one basic exercise: Rear End Under, Front End Across.

The tips I'm sharing are the oldest exercises known between horse and man. Secular history and religious studies will teach that they were fundamental exercises for the ancient war horse. According to biblical history, King Solomon was the wisest man known to God. A horseman himself, Solomon honored the capability of his army's horsemen and horses by sprinkling gold dust in their manes and tails as they paraded the streets.

Solomon stated in the book of Ecclesiastes, "there is nothing new underneath the sun." The *101 Ranch Horse Tips* are intended to grease the wheel, not reinvent it. Keep our horse industry growing. Learn, use, and share the knowledge of the tips.

Chapter 1

The Care of Mare and Foal

Fundamental training begins at birth.

Give a horse its freedom.

tip 1. Foundation training begins at birth

In the beginning, a horse owner should consider giving his ranch horse prospect a good start by simply allowing Mother Nature to take its course. If conditions allow, let the foal be born in wide-open spaces. The first couple of hours in your new foal's life will have a great impact on his mind, body, and spirit. Clean pasture and wide-open spaces will allow the mare and new foal a favorable place for their natural instincts to develop. Horses are herd animals. The social bond between mother, foal, and the herd should be allowed with no human interference for at least a few hours. This private time between mother and foal is a crucial time frame in the development of the mental, physical, and emotional makeup of the new foal.

A little feed keeps things calm.

Make a loose wrap for a tie.

tip 2. Gain the foal's trust

Two to three hours after the foal's birth, my primary goal is to gain enough of the foal's trust so it will freely allow me to administer its initial health needs. This task will depend greatly on the foal's dam and her disposition, so it may be done in the open pasture or in confinement. I prefer moderate confinement because I like to proceed with tender loving care, or what some horsemen call *imprinting*. I like to keep things calm and natural, using a little feed for a pacifier (see top photo).

If the mare is a little hasty about the human coming near the foal, consider a loose wrap for a tie, as in the bottom photo. Remember that the mare's hormones are in an active state, and a normally calm mare might react differently at this time. If a mare's actions would even suggest kicking, biting, or pawing the handler, be sure she is restrained outside of the pen. Safety for all involved is of the utmost importance.

Introduce the blanket, rope, and other objects.

tip 3. Bombproofing is time well spent

With the many different jobs ranch horses do, they need to be what is called *bombproof*. Imprinting or giving TLC to your foal is an excellent place to start. The foal in the photo is only a few hours old but she has already been sacked out with a rope and blanket. Sacking out your foals in this manner is time well spent and will build great trust in humans. When this foal reaches an age when it will be handled daily and ridden, the dividends from this time will be priceless.

Notice the tools I'm using. My boots are steel-toed: the babies will step on your feet—not out of bad nature, but from survival instincts and not having the best idea of where their feet are. Your language and emotions will be spared with this foot protection.

It is much better to swear by the boots than to swear at the foal. The blanket is of soft cotton. It should be pleasant feeling to the baby. The rope I use is XXX soft and has a metal honda. The XXX representing the soft ply is not as likely to burn, and the metal honda will release quickly if any slack is thrown into the lariat.

Allow the foal to return to Mom.

tip 4. Sacking out at an early age builds trust

Pictured here is the minimum amount of sacking out I like to accomplish with foals before I continue their health care. I break the foal's sacking out into steps. First I place myself between the mare and foal, while the mother is either pacified, tied with a loose wrap, or restrained to the outside of the pen.

As the foal moves away from you, it will return to its mother. Simply keep placing yourself between the two. It helps to kneel down to the foal's eye level as it returns to mom. The foal can see you from its eye in a way that is not as predatory as if you were towering over it. Eventually the foal's curiosity will allow you to pat it or receive a sniff. Build from this point.

Next, I pet the foal all over and consider it progress to restrain the foal lightly. Next, I try to pick up each foot. After these starting points, introduce the blanket, rope, and other objects. Take your time. If the foal wants to return to mom for security and refreshment, allow it. Keep the mother calm: it is her instinct to protect her baby!

First, spray the umbilical cord with iodine.

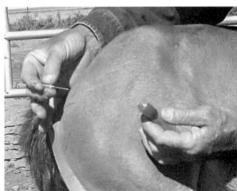

Second, give a shot of tetanus and a shot of vitamins.

tip 5. Give health treatments for a healthy foal

I like to give three health treatments to a newborn. First spray the umbilical cord with iodine. This treatment helps greatly to prevent infection, and it promotes healing by drying out. Simply spray the cord from several different angles, making sure it is completely covered (as in the photo). Then dry the umbilical cord. Some folks prefer to dip the cord rather than spray.

Second, give a shot of tetanus and a shot of vitamins. This is all I do at this time. The foal's individual vaccines will be administered at a later date. In the meantime, its immune system draws from vaccines given the mare during late pregnancy.

It is much easier to give the shots if you insert the needle by itself first, as shown in the photo. Next replace the syringe back to the needle and administer the shot. This allows you to perform a rubbing stroking action with your hand before inserting the actual needle. I have found that giving the shot with all components attached together is very awkward, and I end up jabbing the needle rather than inserting it smoothly. If you aren't experienced with giving shots, contact your local vet for advice about placing the needle in the correct spot.

This is a good time to care for your mare.

tip 6. Keep a close eye on the mare and foal's health

Don't neglect the mare at this time. Hopefully your mare is broke to be handled and circumstances will let her remain calm. This is a perfect time to care for your mare, too. Consistent handling after the foal's birth lets me create situations of trust in my horses that I normally couldn't get away with. The older the foal gets, the more difficult it will be to build trust in the human. Having the mare trust me with her foal is just as important as having the foal trust me.

There is no replacement for wide-open spaces for the mother and baby. However, I bring my mares and babes in and out of pasture for the next several days, for short sessions of care and sacking out. This time frame also lets me keep a close eye on the foal's health (such as bowel movements) and the progression of foal heat in my mare: as the mare's cleaning cycle (or foal heat) comes in, her milk will become richer and sometimes diarrhea may occur in the foal.

Chapter 2

Rear End Under,
Front End Across

The oldest fundamental exercise known to man.

Apply pressure to the rear quarters by twirling your lead rope.

tip 7. Rear End Under, Front End Across

The following tips in the chapter comprise a fundamental foundation for training, an exercise I refer to as *Rear End Under, Front End Across*. The exercise was developed by master horsemen through the ages and it is the oldest exercise known between horse and man. If this foundation of horse training worked well enough to protect a knight's life in battle, surely we as modern day horsemen can draw from its wisdom.

Keep in mind that you will be breaking down a complete exercise into a series of movements. You will also learn while teaching your horse a dance step or two. Most important, your horse's mind will develop an understanding of what you are asking of him by escaping pressure of specific body movements.

As you continue through the tips, I will refer to *Rear End Under, Front End Across* often, and you will see the similarities and purpose for this exercise in different ranch horse jobs.

tip 8. Learn the tools of the trade

A round pen is a valuable tool. There are several well-made panels on the market. I like a pen that is 6 feet tall; a horse will not challenge a 6' pen as fast as it will a 5' pen. A panel made of all round stock will help in the prevention of injury to yourself and the horse.

For this exercise, I want my horse away from me. I use a high-quality yacht rope that is at least 22 feet in length. Keeping the horse at a good distance is safer in the beginning of this exercise, but be careful of using a very long rope at first. It is very easy to get a half-hitch around a body part.

The rope halter is made of the same rope. It is tied in a traditional fashion and serves several purposes.

On my right hip is a knife in a scabbard for emergencies, if I have to cut my horse or myself loose from trouble. I use work boots I can move quickly and comfortably in. A vest lets me carry a few things I can't reach in my pants pockets. This way I have fast access to my tools in an emergency. Notice all the tools mentioned in the photo on page 16.

tip 9. Apply pressure to the rear quarters

Horse training is no more than teaching the horse to give to pressure. The body part or the desired movement that the horse is allowed to use or move in order to escape the pressure being applied, makes or breaks the horse's understanding of what you are requesting.

In the beginning stages of Rear End Under, Front End Across, my body position is relative to the horse. In the photo on page 16, my left hand puts light pressure on the lead rope, urging the horse to move forward and to my left. At the same time I will apply pressure to the inside rear quarters of the horse with my right hand, which asks the horse to move off and push his body forward.

I will create an escape route for the horse by allowing his feet to escape the pressure by moving forward and away from me. In the beginning stages it is common to add a bit more pressure to the horse's rear quarters to make him understand you want him to move away from you. As he progresses, I will be able to ask for the same forward movement by using as little pressure as needed to achieve the same movement.

As soon as the horse moves forward, release all pressure.

tip 10. Immediately release all pressure

As soon as the horse moves forward off the pressure, release all pressure *immediately* by putting slack in the lead. *Immediately* remove hand pressure or any other suggestions of movement and release all body pressure. Move in cadence with the colt. Moving faster than him will add pressure, walking slower will release pressure. Walk with him, at his speed.

If the colt bolts off, throw plenty of slack in the long rope and let him settle down a bit. Gather him up and start over again. The 22-foot rope gives you enough length to allow the horse his learning mistakes. With a short rope, when the colt bolts forward, the slack will be jerked away from you; you will either burn your hand trying to hold him—or lose the lead and the horse attached to it. Better to swear by the long rope than to swear at the short rope and cuss the colt. On a serious note, be careful not to tangle the rope around your feet and get dragged away.

Look at the feet and how they leave the ground at the walk in four separate beats.

tip 11. Walk in cadence

The colt will calm down after being pushed off after first feeling the "pressure." Walk in cadence with him. Let your body pressure keep him moving. Be sure you are on a *loose rein*. Otherwise, the next time you pick up on the rein to cue a specific foot or body part, the cue will mean nothing to the horse because you have maintained pressure since you started. He must distinguish the difference between each request.

Look at the feet and how they leave the ground at the walk in four separate beats. The feet leave the ground rear to front, front to rear. When you start the count with a rear foot, the next foot is the front foot on the same side. When starting the sequence with a front foot, the next foot is a rear foot on the opposite side, or diagonal.

Pay close attention to the horse's inside front leg.

tip 12. Watch the inside front leg

The timing of the feet is essential for performing the Rear End Under, Front End Across exercise correctly.

Now that your horse is walking off calmly and you are in cadence with him, pay close attention to the horse's inside front leg. This leg is the one the horse is going to pivot his weight on as you ask him to roll his rear end underneath his body. If you pull on the lead at any time other than when the inside front foot is on the ground, this forces the horse to be off balance. As the horse takes another step to recover his balance he will push into the rope halter, causing unwanted behavior such as rearing or stopping on his front end.

The horse cannot separate in his mind the requested movements of his rear end and front end if you are consistently out of time with his feet.

Continue to hold until you see the horse's inside rear leg start to roll or step underneath its hind end.

Give him a nice rub as a gesture of kindness before continuing.

tip 13. Facing up

Just as the horse's front inside leg is about to step on the ground, remove the slack from the lead between you and the horse. Once the slack is removed, *hold* the tension but do not pull tighter. By the time you remove the slack, the horse's leg will be in a vertical position with the foot on the ground. The horse will start looking for relief of pressure on its face. Continue to hold until you see the horse's inside rear leg start to roll or step underneath its hind end.

As your horse rolls his rear end under, he will square up on all four legs, balancing his weight. Release all pressure from the lead and your body movements. Offer the horse an opportunity to stop his movement, settle his emotions, rest, and give you his attention. This response from the horse is known as *facing up*. Give him a nice rub as a gesture of kindness before continuing.

This gesture says, "Hey, calm down a little. Be still."

tip 14. Use rest as a reward

If your horse will not stand still and continues to move after he has faced up, stretch your arms out. This gesture says, "Hey, calm down a little. Be still." After the horse has settled, get in another thank-you rub and proceed.

If the horse attempts to move off instead of facing up, don't argue. Continue with the Rear End Under, Front End Across exercise, but pick up the speed and pressure a little. He will like your idea of settling after he has had his own way for a while.

My right hand now is offering a feel of pressure for the colt to step off to my right.

tip 15. Change body position

The next step simply reverses the direction of the exercise. In the photo, notice my body position and how my hand, arms, and the lead rope have swapped points of pressure and gesture.

My right hand is now offering a feel of pressure for the colt to step off to my right. My left hand is now holding the slack end of the lead and is prepared to offer pressure to the rear end of the colt in order to get movement. My general body position is encouraging to the colt to move off to the right.

As the colt moves off, I will again immediately put slack in the lead and continue the exercise. I will look for the colt's inside (right) front leg to be coming down; I will then roll his rear end under to his left and let the colt face up. Finally, I will send him back off to my left.

Walk up beside him and offer a rub of kindness.

The horse is now learning to give to the pressure of the rope halter more from his poll.

tip 16. Teach the horse to lead

By now your horse should accept the Rear End Under, Front End Across exercise. Another step now teaches leading. As you move your horse off, walk up beside him and maybe offer a rub of kindness (see top photo).

If the horse balks, simply reapply pressure to the rear quarters. If you want the horse to stop, allow it and then get in some good visiting time. Next, move up in front of your horse (see bottom photo). The horse is now learning to give to the pressure of the rope halter, more from his poll rather than from his jaw and nose. If he balks, reposition your body to his rear quarters, add pressure as in the beginning, and start over. You will soon have a horse that will lead rather than follow.

Stop and visit with your horse.

tip 17. Ask yourself, "What's in it for the horse?"

As simple as it might sound, stop and visit with your horse. If you take time to listen, he will have a lot to say. Remember that this learning process is not just about you: it is also about your horse. Ask yourself, "What is in it for the horse?"

Your horse has a body, mind, and spirit. Which part of the horse are you working with? Or are you just working? What are you trying to accomplish?

Mental, physical, emotional, mechanical: any problem will be in one of those categories. You owe it to your horse to use all your senses to help him learn. Incorporate your seeing, hearing, tasting, feeling, smelling, and, yes, your gut instinct (spirit) also.

If you are tired, the horse is tired, too, and won't be able to learn well. If you are thirsty, so is the horse. If you don't feel like working every day, then don't expect anything different from the horse. Are you in shape? Did you give your horse a chance to leg up before expecting too much from him? Horses have a lot to say! Listen closely and you will learn about yourself.

Encouraging movement to the right.

tip 18. Gestures encourage movement

It would be unfair to ask the horse to understand the Rear End Under, Front End Across exercise from a standstill at first. It will be harder for the horse to figure out how to move off pressure from a standstill, as opposed to when he was moving. That is because your body and hand gestures encouraged movement. A movement rewarded by release of pressure makes it easier for the horse to understand the reason why he was giving to pressure.

In the next few tips, we'll teach our horse to advance just a little more with the Rear End Under, Front End Across exercise. Let's test out his mind a little and see if the exercises are sticking. I would like for the horse to show some mental and physical advancement by beginning the exercise standing still. This will tell you how responsive the horse really is to the rope halter and lead.

Move your body into position just off the horse's hip.

tip 19. Try the exercise from a standstill

Lift the lead rope over your colt's head and move it to the side away from where you are standing. Guide the lead down his side and drape it around and behind his hindquarters. Move your body into position just off the horse's hip and hold light pressure on the lead rope (see photo).

We want the horse to escape the lateral pressure being applied to his face by moving his rear end under.

Be sure you have done all your colt's sacking-out homework before you attempt this exercise. If you are working with an older horse not used to rope work, I would suggest that you round-pen him and sack him out first. When the lead rope is put over the horse's head and laid on the other side of a horse that will not accept the lead rope, there stands a good chance he'll jump on you for security.

Continue to hold up your hand as though you are pulling on his eye.

tip 20. Pulling on an eye

The next step comes from the cowboy expression *pulling on an eye*. As the colt starts to move off pressure from the lead and rope halter, stand still and let the horse do the work. The horse will pivot on his front end while rolling his rear end under. The rear feet will move differently from a standstill, as opposed to when the horse's body is already in motion. As your horse makes this movement, reward him by putting slack in the lead. Continue to hold your hand up as though you are pulling on his eye.

In time, it will not be long until you can pull on the horse's eye using your hand only, getting your horse to step around without using the lead rope.

Swap hand positions on the lead.

tip 21. Ask for both steps of the dance

The next tip is actually a choice of the handler. As the colt rolls his hindquarters from the standstill, your body will be in a perfect place to offer the horse a chance to bring the front end across. As the colt comes around, or under, with his rear end, swap hand positions on the lead. Offer the colt a feel of pressure from your front or leading hand to move off in the opposite direction. Your rear hand will offer a gesture of pressure to move off, too. This choice is seen in the photo.

The other choice is to let the colt face up and give him a good-job rub or two. Personally, I like to let the colt face up a few times and reward him before I ask for both steps of the dance.

Remove the predator pressure from the horse's top trifocal vision.

tip 22. Point to the ground and lower his head

All movement so far has been forward or lateral. To advance your horse, the next step will teach him to drop his head down using vertical motion. This step will enable you to help your horse break at the poll and back up at an easier time.

I first kneel down (providing I'm around a gentle horse) to remove that predator pressure from the horse's top trifocal vision. Next I take firm hold on the bottom of the halter and shake it with firmness, without jerking or slack-pulling. I'm politely aggravating the horse, so to speak.

At the first glimpse or feel of give (downward movement), I release the pressure immediately. I continue to do this until the colt drops his head to the ground (see photo).

A horseman can eventually point to the ground and get the horse to lower his head.

Accept the slightest movement or shift of weight backwards.

tip 23. Backing up

Let's back up just a little. After you have taught your horse to drop his head by giving pressure to the rope halter, stand by his side and continue to hold that pressure. We are now looking for our horse to escape the pressure being applied by moving backward.

To make it simple, I will accept the slightest movement or shift of weight backward. To put it in cowboy terms, "Before God gets the news the colt offered to back up." I will then release the pressure from the lead.

Preparing them for the real world.

tip 24. Colts should lead anywhere

Your colts and horses should lead anywhere now. Let's lead our horses out of this pen and put some of these exercises to work on the obstacle course. We will be preparing the horses for the real world, if they are going to become ranch horses.

After the ground exercises have been established in your horse's mind, you will have a tool at your immediate disposal to use in further training: the Rear End Under, Front End Across exercise. In the horse's mind, the exercise is working as a motivator by asking him to make a choice.

The choices are set up by the handler so they are simple for the horse to figure out. The horse must be allowed to make the choice of performing the exercise in a scary place or amidst objects—or else choose to relax in spite of them. Asking the horse to rest by this worrisome place and check it out will help the horse realize the object is a good, rather than bad, place to be.

Chapter 3

Obstacle Course

Exercise for a reason.

Their instincts tell them they are in a trap.

tip 25. Introduce the predator

The tips in this chapter you will be creating situations that allow a horse to choose between working or resting by the stumbling blocks in his life. If these choices are presented correctly to the horse, you will also be developing trust in your relationship. Horses do not like tight, confined places: their instincts tell them they are in a trap where a predator can attack them.

In the beginning, an open area behind the handler is a much safer place for the horse than a confined area or tight place. When they feel trapped, some horses will choose to run over you as an escape route— rather than passing by or between an object.

In the photo, I'm asking the horse to pass between me and an object—in this case, a safe panel.

Accompanying my horses in many of these photos are my Border collies. They offer predator pressure to the horse. The young colts need to learn to work with the dogs, for they will eventually become a team to work cattle on the ranch.

Lift on your lead rope to remove the slack.

tip 26. Be prepared for instincts to flee

After your colt or horse has passed between, by, or over an object, lift your lead rope to remove the slack and ask the horse to roll his hindquarters under. This will cause your horse to face you. At this time you can either give your horse a rub and verbal comforting or continue with fluid motion and bring the front end back across. Here, I started with a panel, an easy object to pass between.

Be prepared for some quick action by your horse. You may have to *hip lock* the rope (place the rope across your hip and hold tension) in order to roll his rear end. Don't be surprised if his instincts to flee aren't more important to him than your cue to roll his hindquarters. If too much action or a problem occurs—such as invading your space, bolting, charging, or cow kicking—let the horse continue in the direction he is traveling. Make a full circle and pass by the object again. Don't pass by the object more than two full circles at any one time.

This horse is perfect going in one direction, but scared to death in the other.

tip 27. Remember that the horse has an eye for each side

After your horse has rolled his rear end under, release the rope and reposition your hand cues and bring the horse's front end back across, sending him back in the opposite direction.

A horse has two sides to his brain. Each eye affects the side of the brain it is on: left eye, left brain; right eye, right brain. You need to understand that your horse will respond differently on each side. Your horse may seem perfect going in one direction—but scared to death in the other. You will have to teach both sides of the horse. This is one of the reasons why we work a horse both ways, back and forth, in front of the object.

Place yourself on the panel above the horse.

tip 28. Teach from above

Next we raise the ante. We are going to add more "pressure" to the horse by changing our position in relationship to his eye. This makes the exercise more of a challenge.

Your horse might have passed by the scary fence panel and rested there perfectly while you were on the ground. For the next stage in these training building blocks, place yourself on the panel above the horse while performing the same exercise. Continue with the same sequence of Rear End Under, Front End Across.

This must become a good place to be.

tip 29. Understand trifocal vision

This final building block of the fence work ends up with your horse below you, resting and accepting your presence as you pat him. Let him enjoy this; for the horse, this must become a good place to be.

The reason these exercises have gradually become more difficult is due to the horse's vision. The horse has trifocal vision, with each focal point of the horse's eye designed to see different distances. By moving in different locations relative to the eye, the horse's depth of field is affected, taking away from his defense system.

We are asking the horse to work against his nature in order to get him to accept things against his God-given spirit and instincts. This is called training.

Ask the colt to pass through and all around the gate.

tip 30. Raise the ante

Let's raise the ante in the game again. Notice in the photo that we have more objects for the horse to accept. In the fence work, there were basically three: me, the dog, and the panel. Now we have a gate, an old saddle on the gate, two posts and me.

Notice too that the gate is open, which is much safer for me and the horse. Continue with your Rear End Under, Front End Across exercises and ask the colt to pass through and around the gate. Eventually he will calmly walk through with you. Let this become a good place for the horse.

Goblins may be hiding in the midst of a simple request.

tip 31. Horse-eating boogers and goblins

Now let's combine the last several tips in order to reach a goal. Notice in the photo there are ribbons tied on the gate of the prefab panel. I come from a part of the country where your britches would get a little fatherly attention if you were caught sitting on or climbing a gate. So if I'm not allowed on the gate, I tie some ribbons there to let the horse know that he can't climb over it either.

To start your exercise with all these objects wouldn't be fair to the colt that is not used to seeing these objects. It wouldn't be fair to the handler either. So I start with one or two and add them on as we go along. End the exercise using a gate with all kinds of "horse-eating boogers and goblins" hiding in the midst of a simple request.

When this colt is old enough to have a job as a ranch horse, the time you've invested so far will pay great dividends.

When he no longer strikes his feet on the poles or stumbles around, you will know he is settled.

Add more poles, forming a maze.

tip 32. Get him thinking about his feet

Get your young horse to start thinking about his feet. You want him to be calm enough to lead and drive before starting his pole work. This requires working with a different part of the eye. The colt or horse cannot think about you and his feet at the same time, so by watching his feet cross over objects, you can tell how relaxed he is. When he no longer strikes his feet on the poles or stumbles around, you will know he is settled. You want him to drive through the obstacles cleanly.

I start by having the horse simply cross over some poles (see top photo). After the colt accomplishes this task, add more poles to form a maze (see bottom photo).

Work your colt or horse through this maze and over the poles using the Rear End Under, Front End Across exercise. When you are done, you will be able to drive the horse through the maze calmly without him worrying about where his feet are.

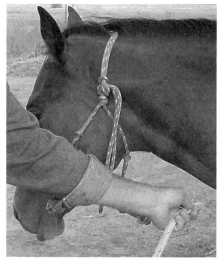

Bring his head down and tip his nose.

He will see the poles
differently as he backs.

tip 33. Backing a circle

Now that your horse is doing the pole work and traveling forward pretty well, back him through the maze. First teach him to back up freely. Start by getting his head down and tipping the nose (see top photo).

Next, back a circle with your horse. Tip his head to the outside, which will bring his rear end to the inside, and ask his front end to move across and away from you.

There is no need to try backing through the maze, as in the bottom photo, until you can back a circle freely. Be patient. The horse will have to change up his foot movement by pushing with a front foot instead of a rear, which is harder on his back and loin muscles. He will also see the poles differently as he backs. This different eye perception on his brain while backing is a brand-new experience for the horse.

This tool is called a **teeter-totter.**

tip 34. Use a teeter-totter

In the next few tips you'll add some boards on top of the poles to transform a toy into a tool—a necessary playground tool called a teeter-totter.

Start by keeping the teeter-totter flat, as shown in the photo. Continue with your Rear End Under, Front End Across exercise, which will be a lot more difficult for your horse than before. Be patient. Be sure he can cross back and forth on the teeter-totter, and roll your horse's hindquarters only after they have completely stepped off the platform.

You will quickly notice you are teaching two different sides of the horse with this tool. As you ask the horse to pass by you onto the platform from both directions, you will find his weak side very quickly. Work both sides of your horse; stand beside each eye of your horse and use different leading hands on this exercise. Mix it up.

The reason I use this tool is simple: trailer loading your horse becomes a breeze after he learns to cross a teeter-totter.

He will paw at the teeter-totter.

He's not all the way there yet, but at least he is on the platform.

tip 35. Let him feel a rocking sensation

The teeter-totter is now pivoting on one pole. As simple as it may seem, this next step is very difficult for the horse at first and will make or break your horse emotionally. It could even hurt him physically. The horse that feels the rocking sensation thinks the earth is going to fall out from underneath him.

As your colt or horse learns to cross the teeter-totter (whether it is flat or teetering), don't be surprised if he tries every shortcut in the book. He may paw at it or step up on it from the side as in the photos. He may go completely around it, dodging the weaker eye, or step back up on the side of his strong eye and brain.

Allow these escape routes—in the beginning. If your horse puts his nose down on the teeter-totter and investigates the platform by pawing at it, it is still a step in the correct direction. The same thing with mounting the teeter-totter from the side. At least he is on the platform, which is a start you can build on.

Make the crossing a good thing.

tip 36. Make the crossing a good thing

The last step for using the ranch horse playground toy is very simple. As shown in the photo, love your horse and give lots of good gestures for even attempting to get on the teeter-totter—most especially when he is on the toy. This makes the crossing a good thing. Your colt has been extremely successful in his mind by accepting the toy, much less getting on it. Make him feel good about what he has done.

Be very careful not to jerk your colt or horse off the teeter-totter. If he accidentally scrapes off a little too much leg hair on the edge of the totter, it will become a bad place to be.

Be certain you let your horse know he was very successful by being on the tarp.

tip 37. Practice with a tarp

Another good item to use in the ranch horse playground is an old tarp. I usually use one that is blue or black in color, but if green was all I had, that would work, too. In the photo, the poles on the tarp are there mostly for weight. (When this photo was taken, the wind was blowing around 25 mph; trust me, a moving tarp and a still tarp are two different things to a horse.)

You are working with the horse's eye again. A horse has trouble with depth perception, which is why some horses have trouble crossing water. They think the earth is going to fall out from underneath them. The tarp simulates this same effect to the horse's eye. Be satisfied if the horse will get on only part of the tarp in the beginning. Be certain you let your horse know he was very successful by being on the tarp.

I know about people losing events due to a blowing tarp in the horse show arena. Your ranch horse playground can keep that from happening to you.

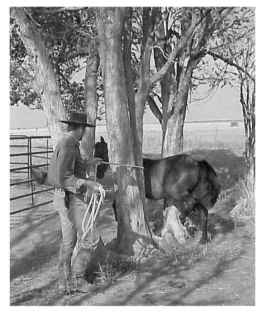

Take your long rope and lay it on the tree trunk.

tip 38. Have a few good trees

In your ranch horse playground, there should be some snubbing posts or a few good trees. These trees play several roles. Not only are they obstacles, but they also act as self-motivators for horses that won't give you their face. Using a patch of trees or a maze of snubbing posts, drive your horse through the trees, pretty much letting him go where he pleases in the beginning. As the horse passes by the tree, take your long rope and lay it on the tree trunk. The trunk will offer a small enough drag to show the horse how little it takes to turn his hindquarters. It can also grab the rope hard enough to show the horse how much it takes to roll his hindquarters.

Send him back through just as you did with your Rear End
Under, Front End Across exercise.

tip 39. Create a playground maze

The next step in playing in the maze comes after your horse has gone through or passed by the trees or posts. The long rope in getting a bite on the tree will ask him to roll his hindquarters. As the horse turns and faces up, send him back through, just as you did with your Rear End Under, Front End Across exercise, as in this photo.

Now let your rope grab against the tree as the horse passes back in the opposite direction and continue back and forth with Rear End Under, Front End Across. You will see a lot of action from your horse, who is being asked to go through very tight spaces and big obstacles. When you drive him through these obstacles, expect his emotional level to rise. A balk in movement or spooking shouldn't surprise you.

Make a trail with your lead rope.

tip 40. Train the horse to lead not follow

Now, you should almost be able to lead your horse by a string—much less the pressure of the halter and lead. Walk through the maze ahead of your horse, making a trail with your lead rope. This asks the horse to follow and give to the pressure, instead of just following you. When you and the horse have achieved this goal, you will have a horse that will truly lead and not just follow.

Oftentimes on the ranch, when a calf is tied down for doctoring, I need my horse to listen to the mecate rope he is tacked up in. In order to keep the slack tight from my saddle horn to the calf, the horse himself must listen to the pressure of the rope. I will be on the ground attending to the sick calf and cannot leave my position. The horse must be trained to back up or move over by only bumping the slack in the lariat rope while I remain on my job.

The rope is high and loosely wrapped over the limb.

tip 41. Rope high for standing tied

Notice where and how the long rope is laying over the tree limb in the photo. It is high, to keep the horse from getting tangled in it, and loose.

A horse first presented with the task of figuring out how to escape pressure will push or pull against the pressure, rather than give in to it. One of your worst nightmares is a horse that pulls back against the lead rope and hangs himself.

As I take up slack in the long rope it puts a bite on the limb. With the rope high and loosely wrapped over the limb, I can move my horse back and forth breaking over his hindquarters. However, if my horse gets into trouble, I can release the rope and have a loose horse rather than a dead one.

I'm using a flag in my left hand to send my horse's front end back across.

tip 42. Know your horse can roll his hindquarters

Notice that I'm using a flag in my left hand to send my horse's front end back across. The flag frees up my rope hand, which lets me act quickly and gives me the entire length of the rope. If I were using the twirling action of the rope to move my horse back across, I would lose about 6 feet of rope. Eventually you will be able to make a light suggestion from your body, or even just your thoughts, to move your horse's hindquarters over—but not at this point in training.

Asking your horse to increase his pace here would be unnecessary right now. However, if you pick up speed in the near future, you will have peace of mind knowing your horse can roll his hindquarters and truly give to the rope under high-pressure conditions, rather than pulling back to escape pressure when you are not present. Things can get hot and heavy real quick while your horse is standing tied, but you will be glad to know your horse can roll his hindquarters and truly give to rope pressure rather than pull back to escape it.

I have a wrap on the limb and a bowline knot for a quick release.

tip 43. Tie with a bowline knot

There is no way I would tie my horse like the horse in the photo if he had not already accomplished the high limb tree work. I have to know for certain he can give to pressure and roll his hindquarters.

Notice the way the rope is tied. I have a wrap on the limb and a bowline knot for a quick release. If trouble arises, the pressure will go on the wrap instead of the knot so I can untie quickly. Never think that quick-release knots are easy to untie when they have been sucked down tight by a thousand pounds on the other end of the rope.

Try this on a hot summer day.

tip 44. The old water hose

One of the best tips I can give you at this stage of the game is to use your imagination a little. In the photo, I'm using one of the best sacking-out tools going: the old water hose. On a hot summer day, this is enjoyable for the horse. In cold weather, he could come down with a bad cold.

Use all your Rear End Under, Front End Across exercises and hose them down gently. I have learned that running water down the legs is a good place to start, then work up on the body. Roll your horse's rear end under and swap hands with the hose, just as you did the 22-foot mecate rope. It won't be long until the colt or horse will like your idea of standing still and being hosed off.

Don't spray the horse in his ears or face. A horse's ears have no way of blocking water, as humans' do, so the water can pass to dangerous places. Just let the water run, rather than spraying at first.

I'm training the eye rather than just training the horse.

Travel up and down.

tip 45. Train the eye

Depth perception really plays with a horse's mind. The best way to teach depth of field is to simply change the depth of what the horse's eye has to look at. In a sense, I'm training the eye rather than just training the horse. Here, I'm asking Magnum to come up and down a bar ditch, which is about 6 feet deep. This work is easier on the horse at this time in his life, rather than expecting him to ride me up and down a ditch line when he is three or four years old. If your horse cannot lead down a ditch, how can you expect to ride down a ditch?

Oftentimes, when working the high country gathering cattle, you will find the terrain is very rough. This bar ditch is just a good starting place for a flat-land colt. Use your Rear End Under, Front End Across tool to accomplish this depth of field for your horse.

Exercise is good for you as well as your horse.

tip 46. Go for a walk with your horse

Here is a nice easy tip. Go for a walk with your horse. The exercise is good for you as well as your horse. Go and play, have some fun. Your leading should be down pat by now. Actually, if you have done your homework, your horse is just about broke. On another note, give your horse a job to do and it will make him feel wanted, loved, and appreciated.

Magnum and I will finish our day by stopping off and getting the mail. In my country, that is a good little walk. We learned a lot today. We enjoyed our walk, and we got to visit for a while.

Chapter 4

Basic Round Pen

The basics for any horse.

Moving to the left at liberty.

tip 47. Round pen at liberty

The round pen is one of the most useful tools for training a ranch horse. The term *round penned* defines the procedures used to accomplish having your horse, hook up or face up to you. After the horse has been taught to hook up, the handler can continue with more in-depth training, such as sacking out.

I first work the horse at liberty in the round pen to teach my horse to hook up. *Hooked up*, or *hooked on*, is a term used to describe the horse facing up to the handler. This will be accomplished using the following building blocks.

Apply pressure to the horse's hip.

tip 48. Position and pressure

For your first step, position yourself in the middle of the pen. Have your horse free of any tack, moving at liberty. Apply pressure to the horse's hip. I use a flag to present pressure to the horse. After the horse moves off in a certain direction, remove your body and flag pressure by lowering the flag to your feet and rotate your body with the horse as he circles the pen.

If the horse balks, raise your flag back up and add pressure once again. If your horse tries to turn and go back in the other direction, add pressure immediately and send him back in the original direction you had chosen.

Make a pulling gesture on the horse's inside eye with your hand.

tip 49. Step backward pulling on the eye

As your horse circles the pen he may try to hang his head over the pen, looking for an escape route. If this continues, apply more pressure until the horse's inside eye makes an attempt to recognize you. At this point, you are establishing a pecking order. As the horse gives you recognition for being in the pen, he will bring his eye's focus back to the inside. Remove your pressure once again, and rotate your body with him, following his circle.

When the horse starts to understand you are deliberately moving him in a controlled manner, he will start to seek relief of pressure. As the horse's inside eye gives you recognition, step backward in a straight line while making a pulling gesture on the horse's inside eye with your hand.

Turn to the inside and travel in the opposite direction.

tip 50. Offer a change of direction

As the horse turns to the inside, raise your flag back up, apply pressure to the inside hip, and offer an escape route to the horse—allowing him to turn to the inside and travel in the opposite direction.

When the handler's body movement pulls on the inside eye, the horse may try to turn to the outside of the pen, moving in the opposite direction. If this occurs, turn the horse back immediately. Move the horse forward again in the original direction. Let the horse travel forward a few feet, then pull on the horse's eye again with your body gesture, offering a change of direction. Only allow the horse to turn to the inside. If the horse is allowed to turn to the outside, the handler will lose the horse's attention and focus.

Sack your horse out with your hands and various soft objects.

tip 51. Hook up

Continue by asking for inside turns from your horse. Both of the horse's eyes will make contact with you as their field of vision travels across you, while making the inside turns. When you sense the horse is trying to give you his attention by slowing or stopping as he turns to the inside, remove all pressure and step backward. When the horse stops and looks at you, allow it. Do nothing. Letting the horse look at you is a good thing: the horse will believe concentrating on you is a good idea and standing there is a good place to be.

If the horse continues his travel after your offer, place pressure on the horse again. After moving off a few feet, offer to hook up to the horse again by pulling on the inside eye.

When your horse has hooked up, continue with rewarding voice compliments and begin to sack your horse out with your hands and various soft objects. I use a flag and a soft fold-up blanket. Be certain your horse is sacked out to the point where he feels comfortable around the objects you are using.

I make a smooth upward swing.

tip 52. Saddle your horse politely

Continue by setting your saddle on your horse, gently and kindly. I hold my saddle by placing my right hand on the off side, where my seat and cantle join. I support the fork with my right hip. I make a smooth upward swing and sit my saddle down easy on my horse's back. Don't throw your saddle and allow a rough landing. That is rude to the horse.

Cinch your horse up, starting with the front cinch and continuing with your rear cinch. If you are using a breast collar, be certain that it is connected last after the front and rear cinches. A loose breast collar may cause a front foot to be trapped. You should have a firm bite with the front cinch while still being able to place three fingers horizontally between the front cinch and the horse's heart girth. The rear cinch should be touching the horse's belly. It should be considered snug, but not as tight as the front. Don't leave a big gap between the rear cinch and the horse's belly. This would allow enough room for a rear foot to be caught. No loose tack should be allowed on your horse.

Continue by using the same round pen methods.

tip 53. The horse seeks the handler

Now that your horse is under saddle continue using the same round pen methods you used before the horse was under saddle. The horse will not hook back up on you until he has become comfortable with the saddle.

When you first draw your cinch tight, and when you send the horse off, be certain you are clear of the horse's movement. It is very common for the horse to move toward the handler when first saddled and sent off. The horse seeks the handler for safety due to his survival instinct.

If you are working with an unbroke horse, don't be surprised if he bucks, sometimes violently. I suggest you get the horse traveling, rather than let him continue to buck. Apply the needed pressure with your flag and get the horse moving.

Chapter 5

The Lariat

A ranch horse must accept a lariat.

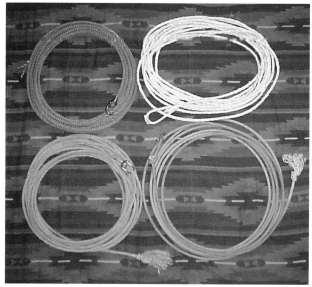

Which is the best lariat or rope for the ranch job you would like to do?

tip 54. **The lariat**

I continue sacking out my horse with the use of a lariat, one of a ranch hand's everyday tools. Different characteristics will determine the best lariat/rope for the ranch job you want to do.

Size, or diameter, is an important choice. The size needs to feel good to your hand. Larger diameter ropes weigh more.

Length should be considered in relation to the job being performed.

The rope's material will affect its weight, wear, and strength. Also, your loop will be held open more easily by certain materials. The choices include: nylon, poly, cotton, and mixed or blended. Traditional lariats were made of leather, hemp, cactus, and grass—long before nylon or plastic poly was invented.

The *lay* of the rope is how pliable it is. The rule of thumb is: S=soft, M=medium, H=hard. The harder the *lay*, the stiffer the rope. The letter "X" before the standard lay letter represents *extra*.

Different types of hondas can be helpful for certain jobs. There are several types of hondas: swivel, rawhide, and breakaway. A rawhide honda will wear well and bite the rope in the loop when the slack is drawn up. A metal honda is designed to slip when slack is thrown to it. Swivel hondas will help keep figure eights (kinks) out of your loops. Tied hondas are less forgiving but hold your loop steady. Breakaways are designed so when pressure is applied, the rope in the loop breaks through an opening made in the honda. They are great for practice shots.

In the photo are the four basic types of ropes that I use. In the top left is a 9.5 metric, 60-foot, poly, soft lay with a metal swivel honda. I use this style of rope/lariat to doctor wheat pasture cattle with. The large diameter helps extend my throw by being a little heavy in weight. If I were to use, say, a XXX soft lay in the high wind, I would have better luck flying a kite. The length lets me rate the calf after my catch, without being in a hurry to dally. The swivel honda helps to prevent my loop from forming figure eights.

In the bottom left is a 3/8-inch, 60-foot XXX soft lay, nylon, with a metal swivel honda. The XXX S and 3/8 combined make for a real good lariat to rope horses in the round pen. The metal swivel honda allows for a quick release in pressure after a catch when slack is thrown back in the loop. This helps prevent rope burns on the stock. The 60-foot length lets me have plenty of rope between my coils and the horse. The length also lets me throw a big soft loop, so as not to harm my horse.

The rope to the bottom right is 3/8-inch, 30-foot nylon core, poly/nylon blend, soft lay, leather burner with tied honda. I use this style rope for heeling while team roping. The loop is easier to keep open when thrown, and the leather burner in the honda will grab and hold the loop open when you lift your slack. I also like this style rope after it is worn. I use it to practice heeling on my burro.

The lariat to the top right is a traditional hand-tied leather lariat from old Mexico. It is enjoyable to use this style lariat for big loop shots. The leather lariat has a life in it like no other. It will almost spring out of your hand, which makes for great traditional big loop shots.

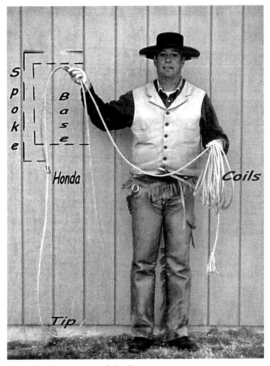

Know the basic parts of the loop.

tip 55. Learn throwing basics

The best advice I can give you about roping is to learn your throwing basics, the parts of the loop, and the different shots to be thrown.

The basic parts of the loop are the base, spoke, honda, tip, and coils. The base is the top portion of the loop. The spoke is the part of the rope coming through the honda ending at the throwing hand. This should be about an arm's length. The honda is the eyelet your rope passes through to create a loop. The tip is the bottom of the loop and the part of the loop you actually throw. The coils are the remaining rope in your off hand.

Your basic shots will be a forward overhand loop. This loop is rotated overhead, right to left, by a right-handed person. The houlihan shot is rotated overhead, left to right by a right-handed person. The thumb of your throwing hand would be turned down in the houlihan throw.

Use a lariat to present pressure to the horse rather than a flag.

tip 56. Rope the horse

I continue with my horse under saddle. I now use a lariat to present pressure to the horse, rather than a flag.

One of the jobs a ranch horse must be solid in is roping. One of the first things I do to teach a horse to accept a rope is to rope him. Young or old, I use the round pen method of teaching the horse to accept the rope and to realize that being roped is a time to rest—not be worried or stressed. I rope my young horses hundreds of times before ever attempting to throw a loop from their back. In this photo is a particular throw called a *houlihan*. This loop is used when your horse is traveling from left to right. By using the houlihan throw my honda will land correctly on the horse's body, preventing him from being hit in the eye. Once a horse has been hit in the eye, it is hard to convince him to let you try it again.

The horse should stand still and allow you to rope him.

tip 57. Show him that the loop is a good place to be

When the idea of roping is first presented to your horse, it can represent a tremendous amount of pressure to his mind—especially on horses (young or old) that have never seen a rope or been sacked out with a rope. Their instinct when something flies at their head is to get away.

Being roped will eventually be accepted as a good place for the horse to be, but it will take much time and effort on the trainer's part to get there. Ultimately you want the horse to stand still with his head in the thrown loop. When you are done, the horse should stand still and allow you to rope him or place the loop on his head, as with the colt in the photo. If the horse moves off, continue with your round pen method. Throw another rope shot at the horse or hold up your open loop while pulling on an eye, releasing all pressure from the horse. Place your loop on the horse and reward him with a verbal gesture and a kind rub.

Pictured is an overhand loop.

Teach him to accept a rope.

tip 58. Develop a neck rope

As you are roping your horse, you will start to develop a *neck rope*. Continue with your roping and pick up on the rope, taking out the slack.

This isn't about choking your horse; it is to teach him to accept a rope. As the horse learns to give to the pressure of the lariat or neck rope, he will start to roll his hindquarters—just as he did in the Rear End Under, Front End Across exercise.

Start by asking the horse to feel the drag of the object.

tip 59. Add small objects until dragging a post

Only when your horse is comfortable being roped should you consider dragging an object. I like to drag just the rope at first; then I add small and light objects until I'm dragging a post. I may start with a dish rag, feed sack, or deflated bicycle tube tied to the end of my rope.

Don't tie the rope hard and fast around your saddle horn. Simply lay your lariat over the horn. This will allow slippage. The slippage will allow you to control the drag (pressure presented from the object being drug). Plus, you can throw the rope away if the horse starts to be upset.

Don't ask the horse to pull the entire weight of the object at first. Start by asking the horse to simply feel the drag of the object. Then graduate up in your training, finally pulling the object.

Keep in mind that the closer the object is to the horse, the more pressure it will present to the horse. Don't present close objects in the beginning, causing the horse to run from or kick at the object. If this happens, you have advanced too quickly.

Chapter 6

The First Ride

Is your horse prepared to ride?

The horse should stand calmly underneath you.

tip 60. Teach the horse to stand calm underneath you

With the horse under saddle, I continue by standing on the fence and performing the Rear End Under, Front End Across exercise until the horse stands calmly underneath me. The exercise is more difficult for the horse to perform under saddle than when bareback. The saddle presents emotional pressure to the horse's mind, raising the degree of difficulty. The horse's vision is being sacked out by standing above the horse's eye from the fence. You are working the top trifocal of the horse's eye.

Practice mounting above and on both sides of the horse.

tip 61. Mount from the fence

When your horse calmly accepts you standing over him, from both sides of his body, set down easily in the saddle. Don't place your feet in the stirrups. Keep your foot next to the fence on a rail. This will allow you to step onto the fence and up off the horse if the horse becomes nervous. Practice mounting above and on both sides of the horse.

Make exaggerated movements in the saddle. This will help your horse become accustomed to the movement, noise, and weight of the saddle with rider. Give your horse many rubs of kindness and nice verbal gestures. Slap your saddle leather, making exaggerated noises.

Never mount a horse that is not standing still.

tip 62. Never mount a horse that is not standing still

I continue by teaching my horse to accept me mounting from the ground. I jump up and down beside my horse's head until he remains calm with my body gesture. Next, I place my foot in the stirrup—providing I have completely sacked my horse out around his legs and body. This helps prevent cow kicking of the horse for the movement of my legs around his midsection.

I must accomplish stepping halfway up on the horse before considering throwing a leg over and taking my seat. Be certain you have your horse's head soft and in-check, and to the inside, before stepping halfway up.

Your stirrup leg will be straight up. The horse should remain still as you mount halfway up. Absolutely never mount a horse that is not standing still.

Once you are halfway up and supported by your stirrup leg, place your hand on the saddle horn, to protect your belly and face. Give your horse kind verbal and physical gestures.

Accomplish stepping halfway up from both sides of your horse numerous times.

For those not experienced breaking horses, I highly suggest that you pack your horses before riding them.

tip 63. Pack before you ride

For those who are not experienced breaking horses, I suggest you pack your horses before riding them. It isn't unusual to pack in when hunting or gathering cattle, and it's an excellent chance for easy work on a young horse or one that hasn't had many wet saddle blankets due to riding. The weight, sound, and feel of bags on the horse's sides, rear quarters, and back are good experience.

I would be sure to have my horse sacked out real well before I threw a set on, most especially on a young colt. The pack's job is to get the young horse used to things flopping on his sides and to settle his mind.

Pictured is a set of Pandora bags. Easy to use compared to a normal pack saddle, they set over a normal saddle (no knowledge of knot tying needed!). You can pack about 100 to 125 pounds with them, depending on the weight of your saddle. In the picture I have a 5-gallon bucket on each side.

Allow the horse to have his freedom of direction or you will cause an argument.

tip 64. Ride where the horse chooses to travel

I ride my colts and problem horses for the first time in a round pen, with deep loose soil or sand. The perimeter of the pen keeps my horse's distance of travel contained, enabling me to ride where the colt chooses to travel rather worrying about directing him with the rein. Don't argue with your horse about direction: the horse doesn't understand about rein direction at first. Allow the horse to have his freedom of direction or you will cause an argument between yourself and your horse. Be satisfied with introducing an enjoyable ride to the horse.

As the horse changes directions, I throw the lead over the horse's head in that direction.

tip 65. **Follow your horse's direction**

As the horse travels in the pen, I ride with his choice of travel. I ride with a rope halter and 12-foot lead in the first several rides. As the horse changes directions, I throw the lead over the horse's head to the inside that follows the horse's path of direction.

The hand gestures and cues that were taught to the horse using the Rear End Under, Front End Across exercises from the ground, combined with your rope and neck-rope work, will benefit you at this time.

Chapter 7

Hobbles and a Feedbag

Some advice from a man that has been left on foot.

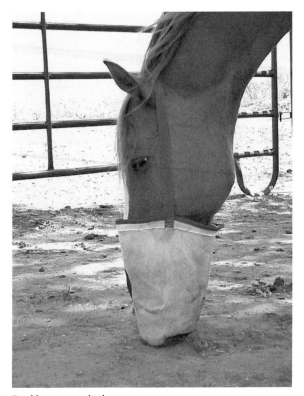

Food is a way to the heart.

tip 66. Horses eat with their head down

Food is a way to the heart (a horse is much like a human in this respect). Making your own feedbag can be very rewarding. Although there are several nice bags available on the market, I use a heavy canvas for my outside liner and a piece of leather for the bottom and for air holes in the front. I use either a leather hanger or a nylon one with prefab buckles; either works nicely.

Horses eat with their head down, which allows necessary fluids and acids produced in their head cavity to drain into their mouth and onto their food for proper digestion.

The feedbag will become a nice tool to use for feeding practices. Feed has a way of being able to make scary situations for your horse a little easier, such as putting your horse under saddle. It isn't a quick fix—just another tip or tool to use.

I wouldn't use a feedbag on a horse that isn't halter broke. The placement of the bag hanger would be the same to the horse as introducing a halter. Plus, the fact of confining the horse's muzzle in the bag would present too many new things to your horse at once.

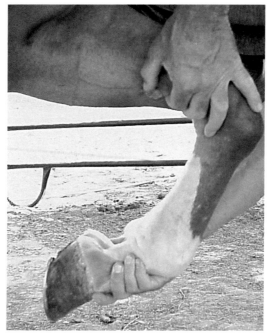

The nerve endings in the chestnut will encourage the horse to lift his leg.

tip 67. The chestnut will encourage the leg

Once your horse leaves you on foot about 20 miles from camp, you will understand the necessity of teaching your horse to hobble. But before you stick a pair on your horse, use these building blocks.

First, be certain you can pick up your horse's feet. If you cannot pick up his feet easily with your hands, you aren't ready to put on a pair of hobbles.

Then sack your horse out well around his legs. He must be calm about things brushing his legs and feet. As pictured, take one hand and pinch the chestnut on the horse's leg you are picking up. Support the foot with your other hand. The nerve endings in the chestnut will encourage the horse to lift his leg. Hold the foot briefly. Set the foot back down and repeat until the horse will freely hold up his foot.

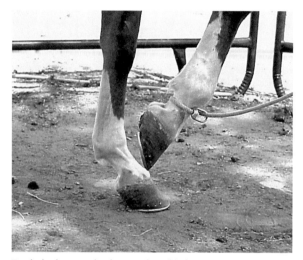

Teach the horse to lead to you from his feet.

tip 68. Lead from each foot

Using a round pen allows me to keep my horse loose while hobble training. After you can pick up your horse's feet by hand, sack your horse's legs out with a rope. Under no conditions should the horse be frantic about the rope. If so, don't continue. Sack out your horse's legs and feet some more.

Use a XXX soft lay lariat with a metal honda with enough length to reach from the outside of the pen to the center of the pen with 20 to 30 feet of coils left. A 60-foot lariat works well in a 50- to 60-foot pen.

Place the rope on the horse's inside front foot and move the horse away. As the horse steps forward with his front foot, take up the slack. Hold the pressure as his foot moves up and forward. The horse will come in toward you, or stop and hook up on you. When he does, release all pressure and congratulate your horse.

Teaching the horse to lead to you from both front feet is necessary for hobble training. I also work the hind feet in the same manner.

Don't use hobbles that will burn your horse.

tip 69. Hobbling allows freedom to graze

Pictured in the photo are the kind of hobbles I prefer to use on my horses. They are of a wide, thick, soft leather. The buckles are strong and built to last.

There are many different kinds to choose from. Large, cotton rope hobbles are good when first teaching your horse to hobble. They won't promote burns, for horses will pull against hobbles at first.

Hobbling your horse only suggests to the horse not to go too far away. It lets horses have freedom to graze, while not wearing their bridles or being tied. Although I have seen hobbled horses outrun ranch hands, a hobbled horse can eventually be caught on foot.

In addition, your farrier will love you. I have yet to see a hobble-trained ranch horse that wouldn't stand up and be shod like a real trooper.

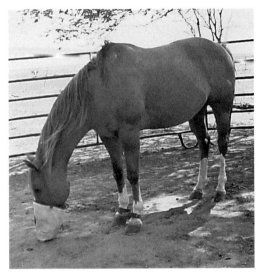

Using a feedbag will help take the horses mind off the restraint of his legs.

tip 70. Use deep sand when hobbling

This step should be tried in a confined, safe place like a round pen with real deep sand or soft dirt. If the horse were to fall and thrash while down, deep footing would protect him from head injury

Using a feedbag will take the horse's mind off the restraint of his legs. I put the feedbag on the horse first, then add hobbles. I like to tie my hobbles low on the horse, below the ankle. Some folks prefer them high above the knee. If the horse stumbles or steps in a hole, the chances of snapping a leg are much less when hobbled low than when hobbled high above the knee.

Just like all other aspects of training, the horse learns to give to pressure—here, in his feet and legs. Don't be surprised if the horse pulls against the hobbles or hops when he first senses the restraint.

Chapter 8

Horsemanship

These basics are often overlooked, even by professionals.

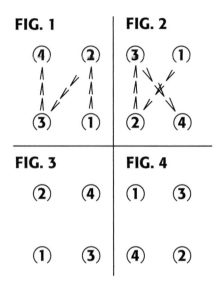

The feet leave the ground rear to front, front to rear.

tip 71. The four-beat walk

Knowing a horse's footfall at each gait is essential. First let's take a look at the four-beat walk. The diagram will teach us the sequence of the horse's feet.

In figure 1, the first foot to leave the ground is the right rear #1. The next foot to leave the ground is the right front #2, followed by the left rear #3, ending with the left front #4.

In figure 2, the count starts with a front foot. The first foot to leave the ground is the right front #1. The next foot is the left rear #2, followed by the left front #3. The last foot is the right rear #4.

The key to understanding the sequence is when you start counting with a rear foot, the next foot in the count is the front foot on the same side. If you start counting with a front foot, the next foot in the count is the rear foot on the opposite side or (on the diagonal). The feet leave the ground rear to front, front to rear, regardless of where you are in your count.

Alternating
Left & Right Leg Aids

Ride with loose reins,
leave the horse's
head alone.

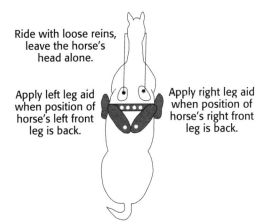

Apply left leg aid
when position of
horse's left front
leg is back.

Apply right leg aid
when position of
horse's right front
leg is back.

Pick the life up in your body for a faster walk.
Take the life out of your body for a slower walk.

The horse's feet are your feet.

tip 72. Time your leg cues with the horse's individual step

I teach my horses to move out or slow down by responding to my seat and leg cues. As the horse starts to take an individual step with its front foot at the walk, I press against his side with my leg, around the top of my calf. A faster step requires more pressure or more life from your body. A slower step has less pressure or less life from your body.

I then alternate my leg cues at each individual step as I ride, marching, so to speak—left-right, left-right. As the horse is walking forward, apply your leg cues when the horse's front legs are moving backward, in the straight-up vertical position. This tip will place your leg cues in approximate time with the horse's leg movement. Remember! The horse's feet are your feet.

Two-Beat Trot

Diagonals
Left and Right

Beats One
and Two

(L) (R)   (2) (1)

(R) (L)   (1) (2)

The feet lift and land together
on two separate beats of diagonals.
1st set–2nd set. The left rear works with
the right front. The right rear works
with the left front.
When we call off a certain diagonal
left or right, we are referring to the
front leg in the pair working together.

"Rise and fall with the shoulder on the wall."

tip 73. Rise and fall with the shoulder on the wall

A handy little rhyme that helped me understand my body position while posting at the trot is, "Rise and fall with the shoulder on the wall." What that means is, if you were traveling to the left in an arena, your horse's outside shoulder (the one toward the wall or rail) would be your right. The two feet moving simultaneously here—the right front and left rear—are considered the horse's right diagonal; we are timing our body movement with the horse's right front shoulder and the left rear hip.

Rise and fall means lift your seat up as the horse's working pair of legs leave the ground. As a visual aid, when the horse's outside shoulder is back as far as it can go, the moment it lifts to travel forward, lift your seat with the forward travel of the horse. As the shoulder steps down in stride, sit down.

In conclusion, when posting to the left, time yourself with the horse's right diagonal. When posting to the right, time yourself with the left diagonal.

Foot Fall
The Lope

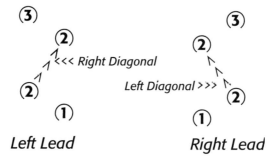

Left Lead

Right Lead

Two sets of legs, each has a leading leg.

tip 74. Imagine the lope as a front and rear set of legs

Don't make the lope difficult. Look at it as having two sets of legs: a front set and a rear set. The horse has a leading leg in each set (see diagram). The horse travels naturally with his leading legs to the inside of the direction you are riding. When loping to the left, for example, the horse's leading leg in each set would be the left. The leading leg will be the one in each set that is reaching the furthest distance in stride. If you are riding in the improper lead, your horse will be uncomfortable and off balance.

Be sure your hands are in time with your horse's head as it travels up and down. As the horse's head and ears go up and down, so should your hand and seat. This will keep you from accidentally sending stop messages to the horse. A rider who is out of time will bump against the horse's face and stop the forward movement. In time, your hand cue will mean nothing to the horse. This is also where speed control comes into play: Hand and seat forward means more speed; hand and seat back means less speed.

The front cue is behind the front cinch.

The rear cue is in front of the rear cinch.

tip 75. Use a set of cues

It is very important to instill in your horse's mind a set of cues that separate his rear end from his front end, so be very particular about where you place your leg aids and cues.

For my front end cue, I place my spur or boot heel just behind the front cinch. For my rear cue, I place the cue just in front of the rear cinch (see photos).

In the beginning, your horse will push against the cue pressure instead of giving to it. Be patient, and as soon as the horse moves off the cue, remove the pressure. Always try to use less pressure to teach your horse. Once the horse learns the cues, let the horse know you have a spur to use rather than one you use all the time.

Move the front end to the left with the right leg cue.

Move the rear end to the left with the right leg cue.

tip 76. Teach the horse to move on a diagonal

This tip will help you with your lead departures, spins, and everyday ranch work such as opening a gate. Teach your horse to move each quarter to the left and to the right.

This will be accomplished by moving him forward at the walk while applying the leg cues. You may have to capture the horse's face slightly (or maintain light contact) in the beginning to prevent him from blowing out forward when the cues are first introduced.

The top photo shows the horse moving its front end to the left, known as *drifting* or *coming on the diagonal*. The bottom photo shows the horse's rear end moving to the left, called *haunches in* or *two-tracking*.

Be accurate with your cue placement. Mix your training aids up for the horse. Walk forward, tuck your horse for a few strides, release his face, walk forward at liberty, ask your horse to tuck, move his front end or rear end, release his face, walk forward at liberty. Stop, rest.

Chapter 9

The Gate

Mandatory knowledge for a ranch horse.

Start by walking through an open gate.

tip 77. Pass through an open gate first

Being able to open a gate from a horse's back is a mandatory job for a ranch horse. A good place to introduce your horse to this experience is with a gate set up in an obstacle course. It is desirable and safer if the gate is free swinging and free of fence attachments. Start by simply walking through the open gate. Reaching down and gently swinging the gate as you pass through is a good place to start, too; but if your horse is a little spooked by you reaching down, be satisfied at first by just passing through. Horses are naturally afraid of tight places.

Accomplish passing through an open gate before opening a closed gate. Be sure your horse fully understands your hand and leg cues before attempting this task.

Your horse should remain still while you open the gate latch.

tip 78. Rattle the gate and latch before opening

Next, ride near a closed gate and open the latch. As your horse stops by the gate, rattle the gate and latch to determine if your horse will handle the pressure of noise and entrapment.

Your horse should remain still while you open the gate latch. If your horse will not accept the pressure of being next to the gate, put him to work in a safe place and manner. Once you sense he's tired slightly and his attention has returned to you, return to the gate—offering the horse a place of rest while you rattle the gate and open the latch.

You will use your leg cues to ask the horse to quarter into, and or side-pass, near the gate. Your horse's position should be situated lateral to the gate.

Keep your gate-side hand on the gate corner.

tip 79. Keep your gate-side hand on the corner

As you open the gate to your right, place your left leg, which is your front-end leg cue, on the horse, asking him to move his front end directly into the gate. Your gate-side or right leg will remain neutral with slight side contact supporting the horse.

Keep your gate-side or right hand on the gate corner. This hand placement will act as your pivot point as you create an opening to walk your horse through. Ask the horse to move calmly forward as you continue to hold the gate. Hold the reins in your left hand, giving your horse direction and support. Don't let your horse blow through the opening.

Sometimes when riding a horse that is new to opening gates, if the horse shows a high level of resistance passing through, remove your hand from the gate and push the gate open with your gate-side leg, relieving the pressure of the gate from the horse. Be sure there is a wide enough opening to pass safely through the gate.

Do not to carry or wear any items on yourself, your horse, or your tack that could catch on the gate, in case your horse decides to bolt through the opening.

As you walk your horse through the gate opening, swap your leg cues.

tip 80. Position to the gate determines your cues

As you walk your horse through the gate opening, swap your leg cues. Your left leg—which had been moving your horse diagonally forward to the right—will now go to neutral and support the horse's front end, preventing it from excessive movement but allowing it to pivot. Your gate-side or right leg will now change from support to a rear end cue, asking the horse to move his rear quarters over to the left.

Your hand cues remain the same.

Place your left leg cue on the horse's left side, between the front and rear cinch.

tip 81. **Close the latch**

As your horse passes his hindquarters through the gate opening and clears the gate post, he will be parallel to gate.

Remove your leg cues. Sit down in your seat. Pick up on the reins with your left hand, as light as possible, asking the horse to stop all movement. Release all cues, relax, sit quietly.

Now, place your left leg cue to the horse's left side, between the front and rear cinch. At the same time remove your right leg cue and allow your horse to move right, toward the gate.

As your horse side-passes to the right, your left hand controls the reins. Your right hand continues to hold and push the gate. Your rein aids should allow the horse to move laterally toward the gate while at the same time preventing any forward movement.

When the horse is still and calm, close the gate latch.

Chapter 10

Working Livestock

Ranch horses need a job.

Mirror image every move the calf makes.

tip 82. Use a mechanical calf

To offset the cost of working and maintaining live cattle, I use a mechanical calf as a training aid. The remote device gives me complete control of the calf's speed and direction. With this piece of equipment, I introduce the idea of cutting to the ranch horse.

My goal is to have my horse make a mirror image of every move the calf makes. I begin by riding in the same direction as the calf, keeping my horse at a distance of approximately 15 feet to the side of the calf and positioning my horse's head perpendicular to the calf's shoulder.

The horse's emotions and flight instinct can be affected greatly when first introduced to a mechanical calf. The closer your horse is to the device, the more pressure it will present. When the calf first moves, look for additional pressure.

As the calf stops, maintain the horse's position to the calf, and stop straight.

tip 83. Tracking and rating

Maintaining a particular position and distance between the horse and calf is called *tracking*. Tracking the calf at different speeds while keeping the horse in position is called *rating*.

As the calf stops, maintain the horse's position to the calf and stop straight. As your calf turns back in the opposite direction, ask your horse to turn back with the calf and resume his tracking position. When changing directions, also practice turning the calf halfway around and stop. This places the calf and horse nose to nose. This position teaches the horse that he held the calf. With the calf still, move your horse toward the calf, then move the calf. This maneuver teaches the horse to challenge and control the calf. With the calf still and facing the horse, back your horse up, then move the calf. This maneuver teaches your horse that he can draw the calf into movement.

As your horse learns his maneuvers, use fewer human cues and allow the calf to stop and turn the horse.

Always keep your horse focused on the calf. Never remove the horse's vision from the calf when changing directions.

The horse will learn to turn with the calf on his own.

tip 84. Stop your horse straight

To build class and form in your horse, consider the following. First teach your horse to track and rate the calf at a consistent slow speed. Keep things slow and simple. Continue by alternating the calf's traveling distance, stops, stop locations, turns, and tracking speed.

As you stop your horse, be certain he stops straight. Don't allow the horse to shoulder in toward the calf as he learns to anticipate the calf's stop and change of direction. If the horse goes past the calf as he stops, correct him—don't punish him. Back him up to his proper position and let him rest and focus on the stopped calf.

Your horse will eventually start watching, stopping, and turning with the calf on his own. Give him great praise for the slightest effort. Never let the horse know he made a mistake, or lost a calf. Work in short sessions.

tip 85. Building a round-and-round

On our ranch we also use a burro to teach our horses to track and rate stock. The burro is relatively inexpensive while serving a useful purpose and living a good life. I tie the halter-broke burro to what I call a *round-and-round*.

I build a round-and-round by tamping a stationary 8-foot section of 3 3/4-inch diameter pipe approximately 4 feet, vertically into the ground. From a 4-inch diameter pipe I cut and weld a ring collar 2 inches wide onto the 3 3/4-inch diameter stationary pipe. Weld the ring collar 3 feet from the top of the stationary pipe, leaving about 1 foot of clearance between the ring and the ground. Place a 3-foot piece of 4-inch diameter pipe over the stationary pipe, which rests and pivots on the welded ring collar. Weld onto the 4-inch overlaying pipe a horizontal arm made from a 20-foot section of 1 1/2-inch pipe. Then weld a support rod connected from the end of the horizontal pipe arm back to the 4-inch overlaying pipe made of 1/2-inch round stock. At the ends of the horizontal extension arm and support rod, weld a ring large enough for a lead rope to pass through. Use a heavy walled schedule of pipe.

To begin tracking the burro, ask your horse to place his nose just behind, and to the left of the burro's left hip. It is important to place your horse so you can clearly see both hind legs of the burro. You can only rope what you see. When the burro moves off from the pressure of the horse, ask your horse to track and rate.

Ask your horse to track and rate.

A trap shot.

tip 86. **Throw the trap shot**

Now we will rope the burro by its hind legs. This is called *heeling*, an excellent exercise for ranch horses.

Be certain you have done all your homework before trying this tip. Your horse must be bombproof from the rope, and you must be handy with the lariat.

As you track and begin to swing your loop, expect the burro to move faster. Continue to track and rate the burro while swinging your loop in time with the burro's hind legs (as the burro's legs are back, the tip of your loop should be crossing over the burro's back). Throw your trap shot (a specific loop to catch heels). After you have thrown your shot on the burro, whether you catch the heels or not, stop your horse, remove the slack in the rope, go to the horn, and pretend to dally. The horse will soon learn to stop on his own after he sees the rope has been thrown.

Don't pull your rope tight on the burro's legs. If you burn his legs with the rope, he won't work for you for very long. Be careful no exercise is worth the price of your fingers or life.

Chapter 11

Catch Line and Knots

Every horseman should know these knots.

A catch line.

tip 87. Build a catch line

After your horses have been successful at the preceding tips, here is a good one for you. Some people call this a *war bridle*. I don't want a war with my horse so I don't think in that manner; I call it a *catch line*. Be very sure your horse can respect a neck rope, knows his groundwork, and can be led before using this handy deal. Otherwise you will have a horse dragging you off.

I use a small-diameter, soft yacht rope for this catch line. This rope is handy to have in your pocket. I have found that it is a little easier to catch your horse with a catch line than a halter and lead, which signals work to him.

In the photo, notice the bowline knot at the bottom of the horse's throatlatch. This knot will not slip. After the bowline knot is tied around the neck, make two double hitches. Place one over the horse's poll and the other over his nose.

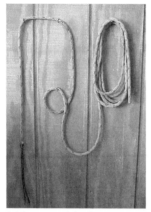

A. The parts of the knot.

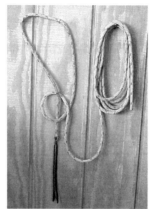

B. Place the tail of your rope through the number nine.

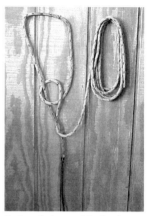

C. Over in front of the lead.

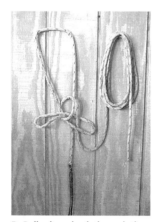

D. Pull a loop back through the number nine.

E. Pull your ends tight. The knot shouldn't slide.

tip 88. The bowline knot

Never tie a horse tight around the neck, or with a knot that will slip! The bowline knot is a valuable knot to know.

I will define the parts of the catch line in photo A. Starting at the bottom left-hand corner is the the tail. It is hanging vertically and has a leather popper spliced in the end. From the tail moving upward to the top left of the picture, the rope turns and horizontally travels to the right. Place this section of rope over the horse's poll. Next follow the rope down to the middle of the photo. You will see a loop; this loop is called a nine due to the resemblance the shape of the rope has to the number nine. The nine is made by turning your wrist up, over, and towards the tail. The spot where the rope crosses over itself, making the figure nine, is defined as a bite. This is the grip of the knot. Next, moving downward from the bite, the rope makes a half moon called the standing lead or slack. Finally, travel back up to the hanging circle of rope in the top right of the photo called the coils.

As you learn this and other knots, it is a good idea to make up a rhyme to help remember the mechanics or pattern of the knot. Face your horse. Lay your catchline over his poll, leaving enough length of tail on the left to tie with. (approximately three feet). Drop the lead and coils down on the ground.

Form and hold the number nine in your right hand. Place the tail of your rope through the number nine with your left hand. See photo B.

Start your rhyme: "The rabbit ran in his hole."

Take the tail that passed through the nine and place it over or in front of the lead, going to your coils, as in photo C. I would add to my rhyme and say "and over the log."

To continue the knot, look very closely at photo D. The tail is doubled over and run back through the hole in the number nine-entering from the bottom, exiting out the top. With your left hand, reach through the number nine, double the rope forming a loop, and pull the loop back through the nine. Now add to your rhyme again: "I reached in the hole and grabbed the rabbit by the tail."

Now that your tail is doubled and through the nine hole, pull your ends tight and form your bowline knot as in photo E. Make sure this knot is correct. Practice over some obstacle before you tie it on your horse. If the knot is tied correctly, it will not slip.

tip 89. Knots and hitches of the catch line

To proceed with the catch line, tie a bowline knot around your horse's neck. With the remaining tail make an extremely large number nine (photo A, next page).

While holding the top part of your rope (bite) with your right hand, reach through number nine hole with your left hand and pull the tail of your rope back out the hole (photo B, next page).

In photo C, next page, notice my right hand. I let go of the top bite of rope where the rope crossed over itself making the number nine. I continue to hold the piece of rope coming directly from the horse's neck with my right hand.

My left hand holds the new loop formed after I pulled the hanging tail out of the hole. You have now formed two hitches.

In photo D, next page, I take the loop formed and held in my right hand and place it over the horse's poll. Take the loop formed in your left hand and place it over the horse's nose. Remove the slack and gently tighten up the rope on your horse.

Congratulations! You have successfully learned to tie a bowline knot and combined hitches to make a catch line.

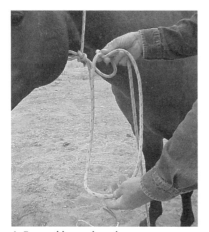

A. Form a big number nine.

B. Reach through the nine and grab the tail.

C. I let go of the top bite of rope.

D. Right hand over the poll, left hand over the nose.

Chapter 12

Tack and Attire

Learn the basics to keep you and your horse
safe and sound.

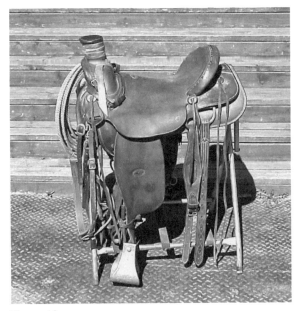

The on side.

tip 90. Set in it, not on it

When picking a saddle for ranch work, I prefer to "set in it, not on it." A cowhand must feel safe and comfortable in his saddle. In the photo is the type of saddle I use, shown from the on side. It is built on a Wade tree having a 4-inch cantle with a slick fork. The horn is wrapped in mule hide for use as a slipping clutch. When working cattle or a young colt, there are times when I want to let some slack back in my lariat, without completely doing away with my dally (the dally is the maneuver of wrapping your lariat around the horn). The mule hide cover on the horn allows the lariat to slip, but hold enough tension to lightly pull when pressure is released from the lariat. This defines the slipping clutch effect.

A breast collar is a must with ranch saddles. There will be many rides on rough terrain, and it will keep my saddle from slipping backward when going up steep elevations. The breast collar also helps keep the saddle in place when some roping needs to be done.

The fenders are preshaped, which helps me when I need to find the stirrup by the feel of my foot only.

On the skirt of my saddle below my seat you will see a loop. This leather loop is for my hobbles that are hanging.

The off side.

tip 91. The off side

In the photo, you will find my lariat wrap on the off side of the saddle. Some folks prefer a rubber band–type wrap for safety purposes; the band will break in case of a hang-up. The leather strap underneath the rope is what I call a *night latch*, which I'm not a bit ashamed to grab hold of for balance, if need be.

The front cinch is made of mohair. This material doesn't rub the hair off the horse and cause a gall sore. I also find I can wash these style cinches by hand, which brings the life and benefits back into them. The back cinch, which helps keep the back of the saddle from coming up when I have something on the other end of my rope, is made of quality harness leather. I ride with my rear cinch snug but not tight. Never ride with a loose rear cinch in case your horse's hind foot comes in between his belly and the cinch.

Learn your saddle; there will be many times when you will need to find things in the dark doing ranch work. The hanger holding my cinches up keeps things organized.

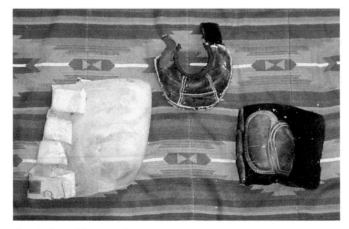

They look used for a good reason.

tip 92. Use protective boots

Pictured are three handy protective items for your ranch horse. I use these mostly in the early stages of training, arena work, and competition.

The gear looks worn because it has been used. But I'd rather see a blemish on the gear than on my horse's flesh; doctoring horses will take the wind out of any horseman's sail.

Pictured on the left is a splint boot. These boots wrap tight around your horse's legs. They give support and remove the shock to help prevent splints and bowed tendons—injuries that will put a horse out of commission for a while, or even permanently.

In the middle is as a bell boot. Its job is to protect the bulbs and heels of the front feet from being struck by the horse's rear feet, which can happen in hard stops or set and turns.

On the right is a skid boot. Notice the padding on the inside and on the heel. It protects the hind ankles and inside hind legs from bumping against each other during a set and turn. It also prevents dirt burning the fetlock of the rear foot while performing a sliding stop.

My fly spray bottle.

tip 93. Keep away those pesky flies

Try this style of spray bottle for your fly spray. First use some water in your bottle before you waste your money on expensive spray. Some horses are real goosy when it comes to spray. The spray bottle shown is my favorite. It allows me to make contact with my horse as I spray. The horse feels as though I'm brushing him, rather than spraying. Most fly dips or sprays will work best if you roll the hair back against the grain and apply the spray. This process lets the spray get to the skin for protection rather than roll off the hair with sweat. The oils in the sprays will hold better on the skin than on the hair. I've tried every kind of repellent the manufacturers make, as well as homemade sprays. I find that none of them work well unless you get the spray under the hair. A little cider vinegar in the water trough never hurt either. Once the horse has a steady diet of the vinegar, their skin will put off an odor that flies don't approve of. The vinegar will also change the pH factor, giving the horse a natural defense system against the pest.

The long rope is one of my favorite tools.

tip 94. My favorite tool

One of my favorite ranch horse tools is a long rope attached to a rope halter. I like a rope at least 22 to 25 feet long, and I use only the best quality as my life depends upon it. I like a 5/8-inch diameter yacht-class rope. Horsewomen may prefer a smaller diameter of 1/2 inch.

The rope halter and long rope are perfect to start a young colt on their ground manners with. As the horse matures it should already be accustomed to the feel, response, and reaction of the rope halter. These factors will make for a perfect first ride in the rope halter and long rope.

The long rope itself can be used for several different applications in the training of your horse. The following are just a few of the jobs a long rope can be used for: mecate reins, poor man's bosal, driving reins, ground work lead, hobbles, and neck rope.

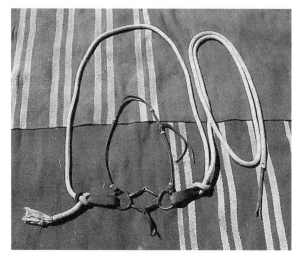

All around set up for starting colts.

tip 95. A snaffle bit is best for starting colts

Pictured is one my favorites, and one of the most popular setups in the ranch horse world today: a snaffle bit set up with mecate reins. The slobber straps are simply connected to the reins by a half-hitch knot. The remaining rein comes over to the side and plays a big role in yet another ranch horse tool. This setup is almost mandatory for teaching young colts, most especially when doctoring cattle. The side rein allows me to direct my colt from the ground, even though the reins I ride with are resting on the horse. This extra strand of rein also works as a lead and gives me enough length to properly tie my horse while in the bit and headstall.

At times, I use a two-string hanger on this particular bit for no other reason than it is handy and light. It also lets my horse learn to pick the bit up on his own. I lean on the snaffle bit heavily to teach my horse lateral flexion. Vertical movement is there, too, but not as demanding as from the bosal.

The different bosals.

tip 96. Use a variety of bosals

Pictured are an assortment of bosals that I use on my ranch horses.

Starting from the left, the first is the mane/tail bosal with a mane/tail mecate. Your hands will feel the sharp mecate hair the way the horse will feel the bosal on their face. Don't use the hair bosal in a mean way.

Continuing right is a 5/8-inch rawhide bosal with mane/tail mecate. The hair mecate will keep a check on the rider, most especially the hands, as it will cut you!

Next is a 1/2-inch soft rawhide bosal. The mecate is of 1/2-inch yacht rope. The mecate size should match the size of the bosal. The bosal size is determined by the cheek sides, not the noseband. I use this bosal when progressing out of a rope halter.

To the right is one of my favorites: the sides are made of soft nylon and the noseband is rawhide. I generally use this bosal transitioning from my 1/2-inch and going into a pencil bosal (far right). I consider a pencil bosal to be around 1/4 of an inch or less. This bosal's mecate is also of yacht rope.

If a horse is soft, keep them soft and in soft tack. Always strive to use a softer, smaller-diameter bosal.

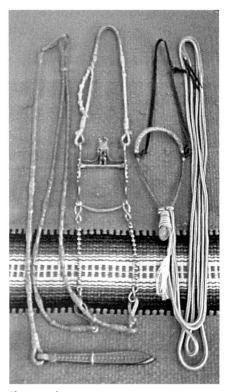

The two-rein.

tip 97. Reins, chains, and romal

The setup for making a bridle horse represents tradition and success for yourself and your horse. The process of getting a horse from a bosal into the two reins and finally straight up in the bit takes years of hard work and an abundance of patience. Pictured is a two-rein setup, which consists of romal reins, chains, and spade bit and a 1/4-inch bosal. The bosal combined with the bit makes for the two-rein setup.

A rhyme to remember about a spade bit is, "The bit equals the weight of the reins, chains, and romal. The romal equals the weight of the reins and chains." Standing *straight up* means the horse has advanced to the spade bit; only the bosal has been removed.

The bit pictured is a Santa Barbara spade. Spades are designed to fit the horse's mouth like a false plate of teeth and lie flat on their tongue until you pick up the reins. Different makes of spade bits produce the desired head carriage. The horse has to learn to accept the spade. In no circumstances may the bit be used roughly. When your horse is to this level, you won't appear to pick up on the bit to an onlooker: you and your horse will work in unison. A horse you have taken enough time with to get straight up in a spade bit will not likely be for sale.

"Handy as a shirt pocket."

tip 98. "Handy as a shirt pocket."

The vest is one of the oldest pieces of riding gear known to man. It dates back to knights in armor, who wore it as upper body protection. Our cavalry soldiers used the vest for general clothing issue up to World War I as an item of warmth.

A cowboy's vest is as "handy as a shirt pocket," as the saying goes. It plays a big role in ranch work: there will be many occasions when you won't be able to reach into your pants pockets. Pictured are just a few of the things a cowboy might carry in his vest: a watch, a spare folding knife, a few extra needles for doctoring, and an extra syringe with another spare needle inside it.

Some boots are made for riding.

tip 99. Boots were made for riding

Pictured are three different types of shoes I use. The pair of boots on the left are Buckaroo style. I wear them when I'm saddled up doing cowboy work. They do a few things other boots can't: They have a spur catch (part of the heel that protrudes past the leather bottoms to create a ledge for your spur); they are tall, to protect my legs and britches from saddle wear; the arch is designed so it slips off my foot easier than one would think. Slippage is a big safety factor, to prevent hanging up in the stirrup (a slick pair of socks never hurts).

I often wear moccasins (middle) when I ride bareback. Without stirrups, the weight of a regular boot pulls against my leg and puts it in a weird position. I can also make close contact with my lower legs.

The boots on the right are your run-of-the-mill work boot. Steel toes protect my feet when I'm imprinting foals and doing farrier work.

Never ride a saddled horse without wearing a heeled boot, and never wear a boot too wide to fit in and out of the stirrup with ease.

Remember the word *wool*.

tip 100. Use wool saddle blankets

Remember the word *wool* when it comes to saddle blankets. The bottom blanket is the key. Wool breathes, even though it is wet with sweat, and will stay stationary on the horse's back. These factors prevent galls.

At the bottom of the picture is my favorite, an authentic Navaho made of 100 percent hand-woven wool. It is woven very tight. Hold a blanket up to the light; if you can see daylight coming through it, consider another choice. Tight knit insures quality and performance under stress. Also consider the size of the blanket: this one can be folded double to make two 30-inch by 30-inch layers.

The blanket in the middle is a three-in-one. It has a wool fleece on the bottom, a felt pad in the middle, and of loose woven cotton/wool on the outside. It also has wear pads for the saddle latigos to prevent wear from rubbing. I use this over a single fold wool blanket.

The top blanket is 100 percent wool with wear pads on the sides. It would be OK by itself under light riding conditions. However, ranch work requires traveling on horseback up to 40 miles in a day, which requires much more protection from your pad than a ride in the arena. When roping cattle your saddle blankets cannot slip. This will cause your saddle to become unbalanced and hurt the horse's back.

Feedlots are a brutal enemy of a horse and his withers. The rider's movement in the saddle while opening gates all day puts a lot of unequal pressure on the withers. Be sure the blanket fits well to protect your partner.

More blankets are not always better: just use as much as is needed for the job you are going to do.

tip 101. Consider saddle fit

When choosing a saddle, you need to consider your seat size, tree style, horn style, gullet height, bar width, rigging position, and your discipline.

I spend many hours in the saddle, so the seat size has to fit. I like a 17-inch seat. I want my seat to have a tad bit of room behind my butt so when I ask for a stop, I can slide back a bit and use my seat cue to aid the stop. The length of your saddle seat is the measured distance between the fork and cantle. Your saddle seat width is the height and width of the cantle.

Different sizes and shapes of horns can be made onto a tree of your choice. The discipline you will be riding will determine the type of horn needed. A competitive cutter, roper, and trail rider would probably choose different horns.

The saddle must fit the horse as well as the rider. A poor fitting saddle will sore a horse's back, regardless of padding. Saddles are built on different styles of trees (known in cowboy terms as a *wood*, which are designed with different jobs and disciplines in mind and made from different materials such as wood, fiberglass, and aluminum. Your discipline will determine the style of tree you use. Most tree sizes will be referred to as regular, semi-quarter, full quarter, and

Arabian. These terms come from the measurements of the bars. The bars of the tree determine how the saddle rests on the horse's back.

The rigging will determine how your saddle is balanced on the horse's back, how the girths attach to the saddle, and where the cinch will strike your horse. The measurements of how the girths attach will be Spanish, 7/8, 3/4, 5/8, and center fire. Rigging will be described as double rigging, 3/4 rigging, flat, forward, and center fire. Your discipline will determine your rigging. A roper would want a double rigging. A pleasure rider would probably choose a 7/8-inch front rig with the rear girth sewn into the saddle skirt.

Consider the measurement of the gullet, the opening over the horse's withers where the saddle fork was formed. An old rule of thumb: place three fingers horizontally between the withers and the saddle. If your saddle is too low to the withers, you will sore your horse.

About the Author

Pat Hooks day-works as an American Cowboy. Alongside his wife Terri and son Zach, they work their ranch in Texhoma, Oklahoma, located in the Northwest panhandle of Oklahoma and Texas. There Pat teaches an apprenticeship program while raising and training their private stock of working ranch horses, Border collies, and Black Angus cattle.

Pat has learned from and is a teacher of the horse. His knowledge trickles down from the legacy of legendary horsemen Bill and Tom Dorrance and Ed Connell. He deeply appreciates the knowledge he has gained from horsemen Bill Black, Ray Hunt, and Doug Milholland. Since the 1980s Pat has given clinics at national horse expos, private ranches, universities, and colleges. His teaching methods have helped a broad spectrum of people, including private apprentices, 4-H kids, college students, and prisoners.

Pat has written how-to articles for various equine newspapers and magazines since his professional career began and presently answers questions submitted to AQHA's *America's Horse* magazine Web site. He has been a guest on RFDTV and has been invited to participate on the new TV station, Horse TV. Pat is also the author of *Fix it Up for the Horse.*

You may contact Pat through his Web site www.hookshorseranch .com or e-mail pathooks@ptsi.net. If you wish to write, the address is RR 1 Box 10 E, Texhoma, OK 73949.